BRITAIN IN OLD PHOTOGRAPHS

# SITTINGBOURNE & MILTON REGIS PAST & PRESENT

JOHN CLANCY

SUTTON PUBLISHING LIMITED

Sutton Publishing Limited
Phoenix Mill · Thrupp · Stroud
Gloucestershire · GL5 2BU

First published 1999



**British Library Cataloguing in Publication Data**
A catalogue record for this book is available from the British Library.

ISBN 0-7509-2297-4

Typeset in 10.5/13.5 Photina.
Typesetting and origination by
Sutton Publishing Limited.
Printed in Great Britain by
Ebenezer Baylis, Worcester.

The official opening of Sittingbourne Heritage Museum, April 1998. (Picture courtesy of *East Kent Gazette*)

# Contents

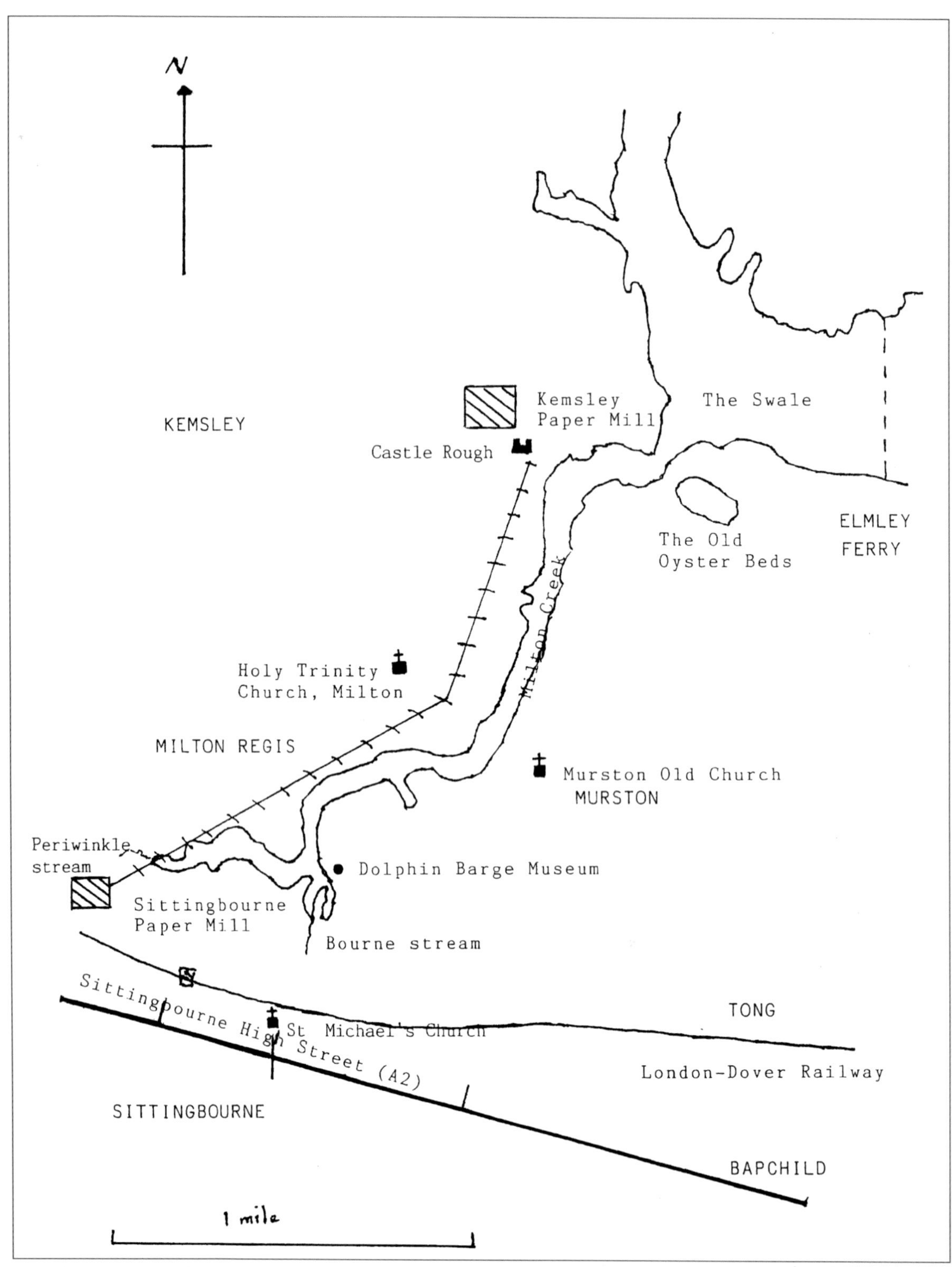


Sittingbourne and Milton Regis.

# INTRODUCTION

Sittingbourne and Milton Regis is a conurbation of two towns which lies close to the North Kent marshes some 40 miles east of London. Of the two, Milton is the oldest, and was, until the early nineteenth century, the larger and more important. To put it into some sort of scale, at the time of Queen Elizabeth I Sittingbourne had 93 houses and 2 quays; Milton had 136 houses and 4 quays. When Hasted, the eighteenth-century historian, surveyed Kent in 1778–99 he recorded that Milton had 5 mills, 5 quays, 32 fisheries, 230 houses, and a population of 1,200. He made no mention of Sittingbourne except to praise two of its inns, the Red Lion and the Rose, which he described as 'the most superb of any throughout the kingdom'.

Milton grew around the head of Milton Creek, a navigable inlet off the Swale. Sittingbourne on the other hand, whilst also located on the banks of Milton Creek, prospered because of the main A2 London to Dover road. It became a resting place and overnight halt for pilgrims, on their way to the shrine of Thomas Becket at Canterbury, and travellers going to and from the continent. But going back even further in time to the Roman occupation of Britain, the A2 is part of the military road Watling Street, which took the Romans from the ports of Dover and Richborough into London and thence northwards. There is a lot of evidence of the Romans settling in this area.

There are several explanations as to how Sittingbourne got its name, the most popular being that the pilgrims sat by the stream, or bourne, to wash their feet on their long walk to and from Canterbury. More plausible I feel is that in the late fifteenth/early sixteenth centuries there were two different spellings of the town's name, Sydyngborn and Sythingborn, which probably stemmed from it being an area of land owned by a tribe called Sything. Alternatively it could well have derived from the Saxon word Saething, which translates into a seething, or babbling, brook. There are two such streams in the town, one following the route of Bell Road and Crown Quay Lane and the other down Ufton Lane and the start of St Michael's Way, formerly Cockleshell Walk. They both converge in Milton Creek.

Another theory, suggested by Judith Glover in her book *The Place Names of Kent*, gives the name as Saedingaburne, an Anglo-Saxon word meaning the stream of the slope dwellers. We seem to have a wide choice of origins from which to choose, but unfortunately none can be substantiated.

The origins of Milton's name is less complicated. Originally known as Middleton, it was the middle town, or ton, of the kings of Kent in the days prior to the Norman Conquest.

The two towns became amalgamated in 1929 to form Sittingbourne and Milton Urban District Council. Five years later Milton Rural District Council merged with that of Faversham to form Swale Rural District Council. There was much opposition to these mergers and a campaign to keep 'Milton for the Miltonians' was launched. Milton suffered because it was one of twenty towns with the same name throughout Britain and in spite of people adding 'next Sittingbourne' to the postal address, letters continued to go astray. In 1907 Milton Council decided to change its name and in view of its past royal connection decided upon the name Milton Royal. When it applied to the County Council for the change, the Council was told the Secretary of State could not agree to the use of the word 'Royal', but suggested the word 'Regis', meaning of or belonging to the king, as a suitable alternative. In November 1907 the change in name from Milton to Milton Regis was approved by the County Council.

At the time of the Norman Conquest, Sittingbourne did not exist as a separate parish; it was part of the parish of Milton. The quays at the head of Milton Creek were all referred to as Milton quays even though they were closer to the centre of Sittingbourne. Milton was the major port, and all the records of imports and exports for the Hundred were grouped together under Milton. It is impossible to establish the relative importance of the waterborne trade to each town. Evidence from the nineteenth century, however, strongly indicates that Milton rather than Sittingbourne was the centre of the shipping trade.

The two towns have developed and grown individually with subtle changes taking place over a long period of time. It was not until the 1970s that major changes began to take place, changing the look of parts of the two towns completely. The purpose of this book is to highlight some of these changes and show the towns as they used to be, compared with how they look now. For this I am indebted to Mr F. Atkins who saw these changes coming and recorded things before it was too late. I am further indebted to Mr B. Kinnersley for helping me locate many of the now long-gone views and recording what remains for future archivists. Without these two main contributors this book would not have been possible. I would also like to thank the many people who gave me free access to their photo albums. Their names are listed in the Acknowledgements section at the end of the book.

# THE HISTORY OF POSTCARDS

The Ash family. Left to right: George, his son George Jnr, and father/grandfather Thomas, who started the family business in Sittingbourne in 1884. The Ashes went on to produce picture postcard views of the town which were sold in their shop.

Picture postcards, which form the basis of most collections of old views, date back to the mid-nineteenth century. Originally they were plain cards sold by the Post Office for the price of the halfpenny stamp imprinted on them and were a cheaper alternative to sending a letter. Private printing and publishing of postcards evolved in 1894, when legislation was introduced which enabled such cards to be accepted by the Post Office for transmission at the normal rate. The size and type of card in use at that time was both smaller and more formal in design. All of one side was allowed for the address.

Later, with manufacturers pressing for more space for a picture, cards were redesigned, the proportions being altered to conform to the Continental pattern, and the law was amended to allow the address to be written on the same side as the

George Ash Jnr pictured in fields where Sterling Road, Roseleigh Road, Downs Close and Woodside Gardens now stand.

message. By 1902 these changes were completed and the front of the card started to carry a picture, sometimes enhanced by overprinting in colour. Many were printed in Saxony, Bavaria and Germany.

By the end of the Edwardian era postcards had become a part of everyday life. They were printed in their millions and the subjects they covered ranged over a broad spectrum. They form a fascinating record of everyday life.

After almost one hundred years, only a small proportion have survived, and today collecting them (a hobby known as deltiology) is big business. To buy old postcards now, collectors have to pay in excess of £5 each – sometimes much more.

Amongst the more well-known local professional photographers of that golden age of picture postcards, whose names you are likely to see on the reverse of many, are Messrs Ferris, Ramell, Wrigglesworth, Shrubshall and Ash. In tribute to them, I have included a photograph of Thomas Ash (p. 7), who started a small stationery shop at 115 Sittingbourne High Street in 1884, now occupied by Midland Bank. He later handed over the business to his son, George, who developed the postcard side of things. As a keen swimmer, George became Captain of the Sittingbourne Swimming Club in 1907 when they were water polo and team race champions of Kent.

It was hoped George's son, George Jnr, would follow in his father's footsteps and take on the business, but because of health problems he was advised to seek an open-air occupation. After studying at Wye Agricultural College he found employment with Mr Austen Bensted at Ufton Court Farm. Ufton Court Farm was developed into a housing estate in the mid-'60s and was where Sterling Road, Roseleigh Road, Downs Close and Woodside Gardens are now situated.

# CHAPTER ONE

# MILTON REGIS

Milton High Street, 1913.

Until comparatively recent times the parish church was the centre of the social and religious life of the English people. There has been a church on the same site in Milton for over thirteen centuries. It's one of the most historic and beautiful churches in Kent, with a tower said to be the largest of its kind in the county and third largest in England.

There is much Roman brickwork throughout the fabric of the church indicating that a substantial Roman building formerly occupied the site. When the churchyard was extended in 1872 fragments of old tiles and glass were uncovered. Further excavations in 1881 proved that a former building to the north was Roman.

It is unclear when the first church was built but it's recorded that Queen Sexburga of Kent, the first Abbess of Minster-in-Sheppey and second Abbess of Ely after her sister Ethelreda died in its doorway in AD 680, less than one hundred years after

Holy Trinity Church, Milton, looking very rural with the lake in front and farmyard to the side, *c.* 1900.

St Augustine brought Christianity to Kent. The porch in which she died was not where the present one is located, but where the tower now stands.

The first church was simple in design. It consisted of a nave and a sanctuary, extending from the present chancel arch to the tower arch in length and from the north wall to the nave pillars in width. The north wall is the only remaining part of that first church. A small section of this wall has been left exposed in the north-west corner of the nave to show the Roman brick and rough flint construction. It is typical Saxon workmanship, probably an imitation of similar work found in the previous building.

The church, named Holy Trinity, could not have been dedicated as such until after AD 828 when Trinity Sunday was instituted by Pope Gregory IV. Two consecration crosses were uncovered by local historian Sydney Nicholls in 1917 when he was restoring the church. One was uncovered at the entrance inside the porch, marking the consecration of the south aisle, and the other at the western entrance to the tower. It is likely that the dedication was given to the rebuilt church of 1070, not the earlier Saxon building.

Milton's development took place largely because of Milton Creek, a navigable inlet off the Swale which separates the Isle of Sheppey from the mainland. The Swale is not a river as many presuppose but an arm of the sea. It is tidal at both ends. There are few less pretentious waterways than Milton Creek. It's barely a mile and a half in length and heavily silted throughout, but in medieval times it was a wide waterway off the much larger Swale Estuary. It is formed by several streams running off the North Downs and converging at Milton.

The banks of the Creek on the Milton side, 1999.

Milton profited from the passing trade of ships *en route* to the Stour (for Canterbury), the Wantsum (which separated the Isle of Thanet from the mainland), the Medway and the Thames. Owing to its unique position, Milton Creek afforded quick and easy access to London, the east coast and even the Continent. This made the town an ideal trading port. By 1649, of all the Kent ports, Milton was second only to Faversham, handling over 10 per cent of the grain shipment from Kent to London. As London grew in both size and status in the seventeenth century, so too did the economic links between the capital and the Hundred of Milton.

There is evidence of continuous settlement in the area around the parish church since Roman times and some historians believe the Saxon kings of Kent had a palace here. Milton, or Middleton as it was earlier known, was one of the six principal Saxon towns in Kent. When William I became king and took ownership of Milton Hundred, it was one of the wealthiest areas of Kent. According to the Domesday Book, the manor of Milton was worth £200.

At the time of the Norman Conquest the whole area known as Milton Hundred centred on the town and manor of Milton, and covered twelve parishes stretching from Rainham in the west to Tonge in the east, Iwade in the north to Milsted in the south.

It also included the whole of the Isle of Sheppey and covered an area of some 17,000 acres. Of these, Bapchild is one of the oldest settlements. It's recorded as Baccancelde in one of the oldest Kent charters dating from the late seventh/early eighth centuries. Tonge was also well established, its mill being mentioned in the Domesday Book. There was a castle at Tonge where the kings of Kent called together their councils in the eighth century. It was quite small and lay to the west of Tonge mill pond.

Milton's coat of arms, a mythical winged beast known as a wyvern, with one pair of legs, a serpent's tail and a dragon's head, is thought to have stemmed from that of the Herbert family whose seat was at Powys Castle in Wales. James I granted the Royal Manor of Milton to Philip Herbert, Earl of Montgomery in 1610. A group of volunteers at the Court Hall Museum, headed by Dr Bob Baxter, were asked by Swale Council to investigate the emblem's origins in 1998 and this was their conclusion. However, subsequent doubts were cast upon this when it was suggested the wyvern was adopted by Miltonians to commemorate Harold of Wessex, the last Saxon king of England. It was further pointed out that the portreeve's staff of office, upon which there is a wyvern, is much older than 1610 – which would seem to disprove the Herbert connection.

Milton's history goes back even further in time, much further than Saxon and Roman times. Between 1871 and 1878, whilst brick earth was being excavated, circular pits some 10 ft in diameter and 3 to 4 ft deep were discovered in Grovehurst. Flint weapons of the Celtic period were uncovered and it was felt the pits were the remains of early dwellings. Many artefacts of the Romano-British period were also uncovered.

In 1869 six Roman lead coffins were discovered behind Back's House on Milton Hill. One had an ornamented lid depicting a lion's head, an indication of the high rank and wealth of the person buried within. At that time only thirty-six such coffins had been found in the whole of Britain and the find of six in Milton was more than on any other site.

Less evidence of early occupancy survives for the Dark Ages, the period from the departure of the Romans to the Norman Conquest of 1066. Some late Anglo-Saxon graves of around the seventh century were discovered to the east of Milton Creek. They were of the type used by prosperous yeoman, or small-scale gentleman farmers.

In AD 892 the Viking warrior Hasten invaded the area with eighty ships under his command, and when you consider each ship held up to forty warriors you begin to see the size of this invasion force. He set up a fortress at the mouth of Milton Creek known as Castle Rough. There is little left today of this once great fortress, only a small hillock. However, whilst most accept this to be the site of Castle Rough, Mr R. Mills BSc, FRES, ARCS, excavated the site in 1972 and concluded that the mound was medieval. He felt the original Viking fortress as described in the *Anglo-Saxon Chronicle* was more likely to lie slightly to the north-west and is now buried beneath the paper mill. However, if this mound was not the Viking stronghold, what was it?

The eighteenth-century historian Hasted saw the remains of Castle Rough when they were in better condition than they are today, and he described them as 'of a

Back's House, Milton Hill, so named after a seventeenth-century owner, Humfrey Back. It was home for many years to the Jordan family who were glaziers and plumbers. Denham Jordan wrote several books about this area. This is where six Roman lead coffins were unearthed in 1869.

square form surrounded by a high bank thrown up and a broad ditch. There was a raised causeway leading from it to the foreshore.' Hasted further recorded that following the arrival of the Vikings, King Alfred marched his forces towards Kent, and in order to stop their incursions built on the opposite or eastern side of the Creek, about a mile from the Viking encampment, a fortification, Bayford Castle. Unlike Castle Rough, nothing remains of Alfred's castle; a house has been built on the site.

The Creek gave Milton a profitable and sustainable livelihood, not only as a port but as a base for fishing as well. Oysters, known as Milton Natives, said at the time to be amongst the richest and finest flavoured of any in Europe, grew in profusion all along the banks of the Swale. Hasted described Milton as being inhabited for the most part by seafaring persons, fishermen and oyster dredgers. Nearly all of those recorded as having fishing-related occupations in the Milton burial registers from 1752 to 1757 were dredgermen. By 1800 the Company of Dredgermen numbered around 140 and was well organised, their rules and regulations being formulated by ancient custom at the Court Baron of the manor.

The marshy banks of the Creek were not the best of places for a town to be built. Its low-lying position made it susceptible to flooding in winter and the townspeople suffered from all manner of illnesses brought on by the cold, damp atmosphere. But it remained a royal favourite and prospered. Milton had been a major administrative area within the Jutish Kingdom of Kent for centuries.

In 1052 the town was razed to the ground by Earl Godwin on his return from self-imposed exile in France after a quarrel with Edward the Confessor. Being the centre of a huge royal manor, Milton was Earl Godwin's prime target. And so the decision was made to rebuild the town on a hilltop a mile or so to the south.

Unfortunately there are no maps left to show exactly where the original town lay in relation to the church, nor the area it covered. The best we can do is to speculate. But it's a fair assumption to guess it lay to the east of Kemsley village, between it and the Creek. The church would have been close by.

The new town was to be built around a splendid new church on the site where the Court Hall now stands. It is remembered in the naming of Cross Lane. The building of the new town began in 1070 and legend recalls how after a few days of constructing the foundations of the new church, the stones were mysteriously moved one night by persons unknown back to the old site where they were expertly relaid. The next day the stones were taken back to the new site, but by the following dawn the same thing had happened again. When a monk quoted from Psalm 77 'Except the Lord build the house, they labour in vain that build it,' the townspeople took this to mean that this was the work of God and it was a sign they must leave the church where it was. And so Milton was left without a centrally located church, until St Paul's was built in 1863 in Water Lane, later renamed St Paul's Street, to replace the derelict Holy Trinity church.

Today the town is centred around the shops at the top of the hill, but between the fifteenth and eighteenth centuries as it reached the height of its importance as a market town and port, it spread down the hill towards the Creek with its numerous quays and wharves. Most of these are long gone, being built over by the new road which serves the industrial estate. With so few landmarks left, it's difficult to visualise how the scene once looked. Where, for example, is Prentis Quay where the portreeve or harbour master's grand house once stood? Sadly it's all been swept away in the name of progress.

The ancient office of portreeve was extremely important as he controlled the operation of the port and the market. It was an office elected annually, and he was assisted by a bailiff known as the borsholder. His staff of office and official weights and measures can be seen in the Court Hall museum.

A similar fate almost befell the Court Hall in 1956 when the local Council sought to demolish it. The old manorial system had gone by the 1920s, being replaced by a more efficient system of local government, and the building lay empty and derelict. The town's last portreeve, Sydney Nicholls, bought the building in 1926 for £75 and proceeded to restore it. When he died in 1947 it was sold to Thomas Buggs, a local Councillor, who two years later gave it back to the Council.

The building, a fine example of Kentish timber-framed construction, was erected in 1450 as the judicial and administrative centre of the Hundred of Milton. It is a rare example of a purpose-built medieval public building, and now forms the

Cross Lane, at the rear of the Court Hall, 1940

centrepiece of the recently completed Milton Regis Conservation Area which includes nearly all the buildings in the High Street. Although the south end of the building has been rebuilt, most of the original four-bay structure survives in a remarkably fine condition. The upper floor consists of a single meeting room with a magistrate's seat, benches and an ancient floor. The peg tile roof is supported by three carved crown posts. The lower floor is divided lengthways: to the east is a close-studded gallery, whilst to the west, a pair of cells. The heavy iron hinged door at the south-west corner is thought to be original.

As the administrative centre of the town, the building was the venue for various functions; the collection of manorial rents took place at the Court Baron, and two High Constables were appointed at the annual Court Leet. Judicial Courts were held every third Thursday and offenders were imprisoned in the cells below. During the reign of King Charles I the building was used as a school, and marriages were solemnised here during the Commonwealth of Oliver Cromwell. Since 1972 the Court Hall has been a museum of artefacts and pictures of Milton Regis, run by the Sittingbourne Archaeology Group on behalf of Swale Borough Council and in partnership with the Sittingbourne Society.

Originally a stone cross and the town pump stood here, later being replaced by a drinking fountain and a horse trough. Only the drinking fountain remains. It was moved to the nearby Recreation Ground in the 1930s and stood there for some sixty years, but following the refurbishment of the High Street, it was decided to return it to its original position outside the Court Hall as a grand centrepiece. Before being resited, the fountain underwent a complete restoration by local ironworks F. Littlewood & Son. Local historians took the opportunity to delve into the fountain's past but no-one was quite sure why or even when it was made. It is thought to have been made by Walter MacFarlane & Co., a Scottish company. When the fountain was stripped, ready to be repainted in its original colour of holly green, traces of gold paint were found on it, leading to the theory that it was painted gold to celebrate Queen Victoria's Jubilee – but no-one could substantiate this.

Adjacent to the Court Hall in Cross Lane are two timber-framed houses which at one time were one building. They were substantially restored in 1959. As they are about the same age as the Court Hall, it is believed they were originally the gaoler's house.

Another building essential to Milton's past which is long gone is the Town Hall, the former Market Building which was built in 1803. The site is now occupied by

The lower gallery of the Court Hall when a new picture gallery was opened, July 1986.

Court Hall, Milton Regis, enclosed all round by cottages, as it was until 1950.

After the cottages were demolished and the Court Hall stabilised, it took on a new role as a museum, forming the centrepiece of the Milton Conservation Area.

A drinking fountain stood for many years outside the Court Hall, as can clearly be seen on p. 17. In the 1930s it was moved to the Recreation Ground probably because a static water tank occupied this area during the war. Following a general refurbishment of the whole town and the creation of the Milton Conservation Area in 1998, the drinking fountain was resited in its original position. Before being moved it was thoroughly renovated and restored by local ironworks F. Littlewood & Sons. As a token of their appreciation for the fine job of work done, Sittingbourne Society Chairman Malcolm Moore presented Fred Littlewood with a silver rose bowl. (Picture courtesy of *East Kent Gazette*)

the former Library, which was built in 1939. Milton was first granted a weekly market by Isabella, wife of King Edward II, in 1319; it ceased in 1878. Isabella also granted an annual three-day fair beginning on 24 July (13 July until the calendar was altered in 1751).

In 1887 the town celebrated Queen Victoria's Jubilee by erecting a new clock incorporating the original Milton Bell, which had for many years been housed in a clock house which stood with a market cross in the middle of the High Street outside nos 68 and 70, the home of Thomas Bradbury, a yeoman farmer, rich landowner and wool merchant.

Like most small towns and villages, Milton had a forge. In an age of horses and horse-drawn transport, the forge was the equivalent of today's petrol stations and garages. It's known to have existed at least since the reign of King Charles I, and in this century was also a farriery. The forge stood on the brow of the hill and is remembered by a small development of houses built on the site, named Forge Road and Dobie Close, Mr Dobie being the last blacksmith. A previous blacksmith was John Grayling who lived in the rather imposing double-fronted house at 99 High

Milton Forge. After many years of service as a forge, it is now an industrial unit for small businesses.

Street, which has survived intact from the middle of the eighteenth century. There was one other forge in the town in Crown Road where a garage now stands. At the turn of the century it was run by Horace Blunt.

Milton has a tenuous link with the author Charles Dickens. At the top of the hill is a tall, unprepossessing brick-faced building now called Burley's Flats. Originally it was Hinde's House, the manor house of Milton. In the mid-nineteenth century John Hinde was one of Milton's principal landowners as well as its coroner, town clerk to Queenborough Council and clerk to Milton's Workhouse. His daughter Eleanor had been jilted by her lover and continued to live in the house long after her father's death. In her declining years Miss Hinde became a virtual recluse and ventured out only at night to visit her father's grave in the churchyard. There is an obvious parallel with Dickens' Miss Havisham in *Great Expectations*.

In 1998 the local school, Milton Court Primary School, had two reasons to celebrate. It was the 150th anniversary of the original Elementary School, built in 1848 on the site of a previous small school, Milton National School, which itself opened in 1821. The year also saw the 100th anniversary of the Boys Council School, which was built in 1898; by 1908 it had 450 pupils on its roll. The old Elementary School became the girls Council School with 380 on its roll. A new Infants Council School was built for 180 children. These new premises were considered to be up to date in every way and were termed model scholastic buildings.

An integral part of the former Milton Butts School for many years was Langley House. It had earlier been a home for orphaned boys, attached to the workhouse, and, before that, the independent brewery of Edward Hartridge, which became Frederick Leney's at the turn of the century.

The area in front of the school, now used as a car park, was formerly the Butts, where locals practised their archery skills in the Middle Ages. A row of seven almshouses was built beside the Butts in 1860 from the proceeds of a bequest of Thomas Bradbury, who lived in the High Street; his house is now a private museum.

Tucked away behind the school is Milton Bowling Club, a green which has been in constant use since 1540. It is said Sir Francis Drake learned to play bowls here. Fanciful thinking? Not really; in fact it's quite plausible. Drake's father was vicar of Upchurch, a small village just a few miles to the west of Milton.

Milton High Street, 1913. (Picture courtesy of *East Kent Gazette)*

Milton High Street today, looking very similar to the previous view. Only the carts have been replaced by cars, and the Town Hall, which stood by the clock tower, is gone. It was replaced by the Library in 1934, which itself was closed in the early 1990s.

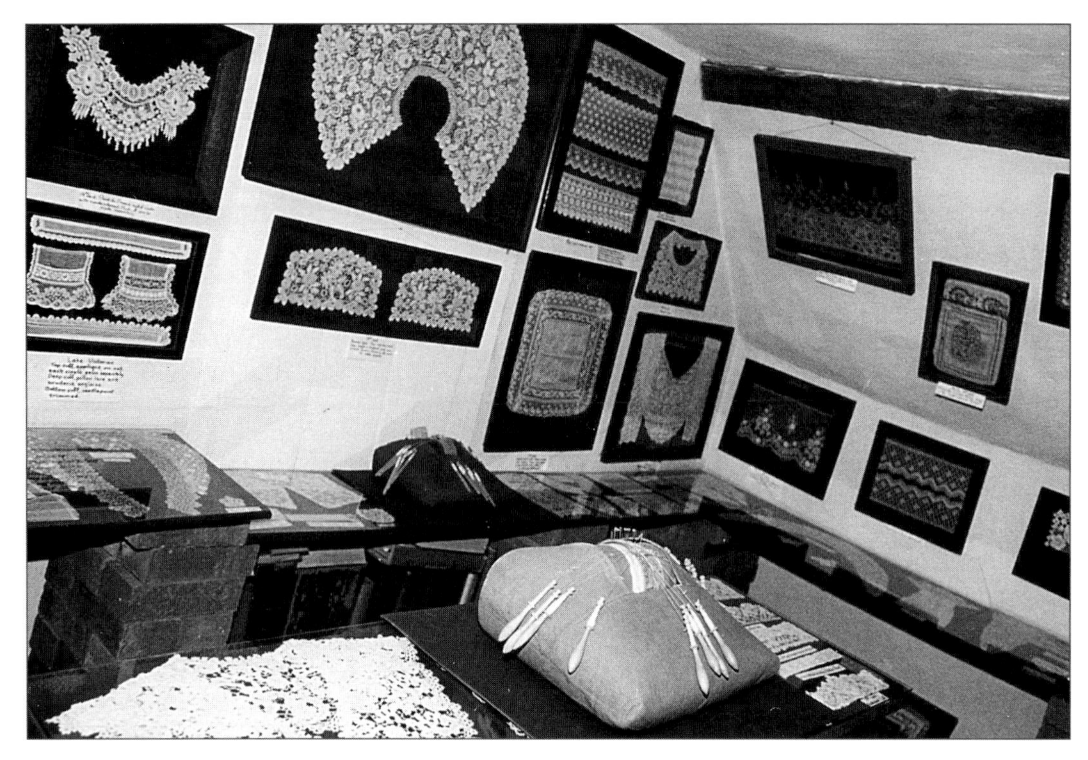

Thomas Bradbury's old house in the High Street is now a private museum of local artefacts and Victoriana. It has a splendid display dedicated to the art of lacemaking.

Milton's cobbler was Albert Louch, who had a shop in Crown Road. Each year Albert would organise a coach trip to the coast, usually Dymchurch, for his customers. The highlight of the trip was when Albert chalked numbers around the coach's front tyre and an arrow on the mudguard. Passengers paid for a number, and on arrival at the destination the person whose number stopped at the arrow won the kitty. This photo was taken in the early 1950s.

Milton Butts School, looking very much unchanged in over 150 years. Only the name has changed, to Milton Court.

Milton Butts School football team, 1947. Back row, left to right: T. Carr, A. Wildish, D. Skilling, I. James, A. Roberts. Front row: M. Boakes, ? Watson, D. Gandon (Capt), A. Graham, R. Wood, D. Belsom.

School Sports Day, 1947. To the right of the picture above can be seen the pre-fabs that stood at the end of Beechwood Avenue on the corner of Vicarage Road until the 1960s, when Laxton Way, etc. was built. For temporary buildings they survived remarkably well.

Class photograph at Milton Butts, *c.* 1951.

A Christmas play at Milton Butts, 1951.

Competitors lining up for Milton Butts Sports Day, 1954.

All lined up for the Grand Soapbox Derby at Sports Day, 1954. Behind the competitors can be seen the Sun Pavilion, which was built in the Recreation Ground in 1936 from bricks and tiles rescued from the old Mill House which once stood in Vicarage Road, to commemorate the twenty-fifth anniversary of the coronation of King George V. It cost £305 to build and was the brainchild of newly elected Councillor Edward Littlewood. Sadly Councillor Littlewood died soon after construction work began and never saw the pavilion completed. The building was demolished sometime in the 1970s or 1980s after vandals had done their worst.

The Meads, a pleasant open stretch of land separating Milton and Sittingbourne, 1905.

By 1999 the Meads as a green belt of land was lost to developers, who have started building roads and houses on this one-time haven for wildlife.

Being quite a marshy area in parts, water was pumped from here to Sittingbourne and Kemsley paper mills. When the pumps broke down, as in the early 1950s, water soon collected and flooded the area.

The corner of Vicarage Road and Laxton Way, 1905. The mill-pond fed a watermill that stood opposite the junction with Dingley Close. It had dried up by the time the Recreation Ground was enlarged in the early 1950s. When a resident in Dingley Close was excavating his garden for a swimming pool, he came across the bed of the stream that once fed the mill-pond.

Today a tennis court and sports hall occupy the corner of the Recreation Ground. The windmill was demolished in 1960 after being struck by lightning, and houses have since been built on the site. The road to Bobbing can still be seen clearly on the right as it goes over the railway line.

Crown Road at its crossroads with Chalkwell Road, Staplehurst Road and Church Street in 1983, looking very much as it had done for many years. The small shop in the centre was the hairdressing salon of Cyril Colchin, and later John Howting.

Ten years on, many of the houses were swept away as an improved link road from the new Creek-side industrial estate was built to join up with the much improved A249 Sheerness road. The Grapes pub was lost in the development, and the Crown renamed the Stumble Inn.

The original Church Street became a cul-de-sac, as the new roadline took Church Street further up Chalkwell Road to where the Grapes pub used to stand. The shop in the centre is a general store, once owned by the mother of hairdresser Cyril Colchin.

Wool had for many years been a major trading commodity in Milton. By 1973 only one wool warehouse remained, that of Gregory & Prentis which stood at the bottom of Staplehurst Road. It was soon to go as the new link road crept ever forward.

The warehouse was eventually demolished and a small close of houses, Staple Close, built on the site.

In the late 1950s work began on a new housing estate to be called North Court, which stretched from the town of Milton to Holy Trinity Church itself on Chas Burley's old brickfield – which had been hit by a doodlebug in the war. Compare this with the photograph on p. 10.

North Court estate from the top of Holy Trinity Church tower.

Whilst the original purpose of this photograph was to show off someone's new car, it also serves our purpose by showing Church Farm in the background. The farm stood beside Holy Trinity Church for centuries, but was swept away in the 1980s to make way for a country park. This photograph was taken in 1965.

The headstone of Simon Gilker, who was killed by a rocket on Guy Fawkes' night 1696 – showing that accidents with fireworks are not just a modern occurrence.

As North Street swings into Grovehurst Road in front of the church on its way to Kemsley, there were just six houses in 1930, one of which I was later to live in. I didn't know about this photograph until I came to compile this book, when a former neighbour passed it on to me.

The original six houses still remain but have been added to. The fields to their right have been built upon and houses now occupy the former agricultural land right up to Kemsley railway station.

The houses of Grovehurst Road looked out across fields and a hop garden to Holy Trinity Church and the paper mill beyond. Today the church is blotted out by the houses of Church Milton estate.

Milton's other main church for many years was the Congregational, formerly the Paradise Chapel. This has been a religious site since 1790 when the first chapel was built. In the mid-nineteenth century everyone had to pay rates to the Church of England. Non-conformists objected to this and the minister at the time, Mr Parrett, made a stand against this unfair law by refusing to pay the rate. His household goods and chattels were seized by bailiffs and put up for auction. The rate had long been abolished in Sittingbourne, so its Non-conformists came to support Mr Parrett. His possessions were bought by them and returned to him, and a collection taken to cover the legal expenses. As a result of this the Church Rate ended in Milton. In 1860 the new chapel was built, complete with schoolroom and vestry.

Like most churches, the Congregational had a Scout troop attached to it. Here's the Woodpigeon Patrol of the 3rd Milton Regis at camp outside Canterbury, 1952. Back row, left to right: R. Guthrie, R. Nichols, J. Mills, B. Higgins. Front row: A. Higgins, R. Revell, C. Hougham, J. Clancy. The Scoutmaster was Bill Higgins: sorry the photographer decapitated him!

Coronation year, 1953, and the 3rd Milton Regis troop entered a float in the town's carnival.

The Congregational church closed for worship in the 1970s, and after laying empty and derelict for some years was finally sold to the Scouting Association for use as a regional Scouts Centre. During building works it caught fire and eventually had to be demolished.

After much public furore and heated dissension, a group of houses were built on the site. The remains of those buried in the graveyard were dug up and reinterred in Sittingbourne cemetery in a mass grave.

Another coronation, another carnival – this time for George VI when an illuminated archway was constructed across Crown Road near the Congregational church. Local traders paid for the arch and nearby ironworks F. Littlewood & Son for the electricity.

Leading the carnival procession is Milton's fire engine, Mary, named after Mrs Mary Maundrell, a Councillor, JP and wife of a well-known local chemist. The name was inscribed over the bonnet. The Dennis tender and pump had been purchased in 1927.

Milton Fire Station. Milton's Fire Brigade was established in 1884 with a horse-drawn hand-operated pump which was made in 1829. In 1901 the Brigade purchased a Merryweather 300 gallon steam driven appliance and, in 1927, the Mary. However, this new appliance was found to be too large for the premises, which had to be enlarged. The two fire brigades, Milton Regis and Sittingbourne, amalgamated into one when the two town councils joined forces in 1930. Milton's fire station was too small for the newer appliances, and has remained empty ever since. In later years it was used as a store by the Civil Defence Corps.

## CHAPTER TWO

# THE CREEK

The mouth of Milton Creek from the Swale, 1999.

The town of Milton Regis as such ends at the bottom of Milton Hill, where the view today is of a sea of industrial premises with the paper mill looming beyond. How very different it all was up until the 1950s when this whole area was criss-crossed by narrow lanes and streets clustered around the head of the Creek, home to a thriving community of fishermen and assorted seafarers. Before delving into the history of Milton Creek, it's important to acquaint yourself with how the area once looked.

At the bottom of the hill today is a wide road, St Paul's Street, which links the industrial estate to Staplehurst Road and the improved A249. Before the 1950s St Paul's Street lay to the right, so named as St Paul's Church was built there in 1862 to provide a more convenient place of worship than Holy Trinity, which lay some distance out of town and was by then in a state of acute disrepair. The brick-built church cost £1,400, the money being raised by public subscription.

Kingsmill pond, lying between Church Street and St Paul's Street with St Paul's Church on its bank, *c.* 1900. This area is now covered by small industrial units and is unrecognisable. This pond is the last one of several formed by the Periwinkle stream, which ran into the Creek at Flushing Street.

Church Street from Kingsmill pond, *c.* 1950. The large house is part of Periwinkle mill. To the right can be seen Hales' butchers.

St Paul's was demolished in the late 1950s after falling into a state of disrepair, partly due to its close proximity to Kingsmill pond: its low-lying position made it extremely damp. The road was often flooded at exceptionally high tides, hence its former name, Water Lane. Fortunately by then Holy Trinity had undergone extensive repairs and modernisation, and was once again fit for worship. Soon after St Paul's was built, a Congregational church, the Paradise Chapel, was built in Crown Road. It replaced an earlier chapel which had existed on the same site since 1790. The Congregational church was declared surplus to requirements in the late 1980s and deconsecrated. It was planned to use the building as a local Scouting centre, but during building works it caught fire and was burned out. A few years later it was demolished, and after public uproar houses were built on the site.

Between the bottom of the hill and the roundabout to your left, outside the old gas works which are now hidden by advertising hoardings, was King Street, formerly Key Lane. It led to Milton Quay, where a thriving coastal trade was based. Corn, hops, wool and fruit were taken mostly to London, and returning vessels brought back all manner of cargoes including manure and household rubbish, which was dumped at the Parish Wharf, locally known as the Dung Wharf. The manure from London's stables and unwanted sprats and starfish were eagerly sought by local farmers to plough into their land. After careful sorting for any valuables or useable items, the remaining household rubbish, or 'rough stuff', was mixed with brick earth in the manufacture of bricks.

King Street, Milton, as the old houses were being cleared away. The railway viaduct in the background can still be seen to this day, providing a useful reference point.

King Street, Milton, with the old gasworks in the distance. Today all that remains of the gasworks is the front entrance, but it is hidden behind advertising hoardings.

King Street, Milton, looking towards St Paul's Street. Sait's rag and bone yard can be seen to the right with part of the Congregational church on the right-hand side. This road is now part of that which runs from Mill Way to Staplehurst Road. Milton Hill junction can be seen on the right.

This was a dangerous cargo to carry as there was an ever-present threat of spontaneous combustion and carbon dioxide fumes from the coke. Remember, these vessels were made of wood. After unloading, the refuse was left in huge mounds to rot down for at least a year, giving rise to one of the several 'stinks of Milton', others including the tanneries, the tallow works and the breweries.

From the brick-making trade, a new industry arose, that of barge building. Hundreds of spritsail barges were built on the Creek to transport the bricks which were in great demand after the repeal of the Brick Tax. In the early 1820s there were nine such barges based at Milton Creek; by 1857 the number had increased to a hundred. The spritsail barge was perfect for carrying bricks. It could be fully loaded in a day with enough bricks to build one average-sized house, and be in London twenty-four hours later.

All the main brick manufacturers had their own fleets of barges, and many had their own yards for construction, repair and maintenance as well. Smeed Dean, for example, were not only the largest brick manufacturer in Britain, ranking second only to the London Brick Co. in size, but at their peak owned or operated over one hundred barges. There were also several independent barge yards which built and serviced vessels for those who did not have their own facilities.

Many of the old barges were left to rot on the banks of the Creek when they were no longer needed.

When improved road and rail links to the capital came along, the sailing barge began to lose its importance as the main means of conveyance, and by the late 1930s had almost ceased to exist. Following the General Strike and Depression of the 1920s, the brickmaking industry went into decline until it virtually ceased to exist, except for the larger concerns such as APCM (formerly Smeed Dean), Wills & Packham and Burley. Following the sale of Smeed Dean to APCM in 1927 two of its former directors, George Andrews and his son Harold, were left with a small fleet of half a dozen barges with no home base. They sought new premises with the idea of building the fleet up to a couple of dozen vessels, despite the uncertainty of the barge's future. They found exactly what they were looking for in the bankrupt independent yard of the Sittingbourne Shipbuilding Co.

The new business prospered and grew with other former Smeed Dean workers joining those who were already employed in the yard. Throughout the '30s, '40s and well into the '50s many well-known barges were rebuilt, converted and motorised. During the war years the company played its part by constructing auxiliary Naval craft. By 1952–53 the sailing barge finally became extinct and the yard became a warehousing site. Some of those old barges still exist, but are now used as houseboats.

Meanwhile, back to our tour of the area. Turning right at the roundabout is Mill Way, a road which takes you to the centre of Sittingbourne. It follows the route of Bridge Street and Mill Street, which was known as Love Lane before Edward Lloyd established his paper mill here in 1840. Running off Bridge Street at right angles was Flushing Street. It led to a tidemill at the head of the Creek.

The days of Milton being a renowned port were numbered in the mid-nineteenth century when Edward Lloyd's paper mill started to establish itself. The demand for water in papermaking is extreme and the natural supply soon became inadequate. Wells were sunk to increase the supply, and slowly Milton Creek lost its natural flow of pure water essential for the shellfish. Slowly it became a silted-up polluted waterway.

As the mill grew in size, seventeen streets were lost. Initially all the raw materials for the mill were brought in by sailing barge, but after the bargemen's strike of 1912 tugs and lighters were used. The mill brought prosperity to some, but was the ruin of others. The pollution discharged into the Creek killed off the fish, leaving the fishing fleet of some ninety vessels with no livelihood. The only options left for the former fishermen were to go into the mill or emigrate. Compensation would have been unheard of. The last of the Milton fishermen were the Redshaw brothers who somehow managed to eke out a living until the early 1950s. They were the last of the Freemen of Milton Creek.

What was life like in this seafaring community? At times it was quite rowdy and could be easily compared with the Wild West of America. There were many pubs and taverns with cheap beer and gin in plentiful supply. The demon drink was a force to be reckoned with in the late nineteenth century, as the majority of working-class people lived in the grimmest of conditions. Alcohol provided a means of escape from

Looking along Mill Street towards the paper mill. To the left can be seen Flushing Street, with the Watermans Arms pub on the corner.

reality. Organisations like the Salvation Army sought to steer people away to a more temperate lifestyle. In 1881 a Coffee Tavern was opened in Milton where you could go for a chat, play cards, but not for money, and drink coffee rather than alcohol. Upstairs you could get a bed for the night. The building stood at the bottom of Milton Hill and was designed by Sittingbourne architect William Grant, whose later work included the old swimming baths, Kemsley paper mill and Gore court pavilion.

It's fair to assume that apart from the lawful trade carried out on the Creek, there was a considerable amount of unlawful trade as well. This applied not only to the usual contraband cargoes of spirits, silk and tobacco, but also to wool. Since the days of Edward III the export of wool had been prohibited in coastal regions. The fleeces were highly prized by the merchants of Lombardy whose bankers financed our monarchs' wars. This particular unlawful trade brought great wealth to Milton and Faversham.

Before the barges came along, much of the coastal traffic was carried out in cutter-rigged hoys. These vessels originated in Holland and were first mentioned in connection with the Swale in 1568 when Elizabeth I gave sanctuary to a group of Huguenots fleeing from Antwerp to Faversham. The use of hoys continued at Milton

The head of Milton Creek looking west, 1999.

Creek until 1905. They were ideal craft to use as larger vessels had to anchor at the mouth of the Creek and discharge their cargo into lighters. By the beginning of the nineteenth century, however, new deeper water wharfage was established on the opposite bank at Murston.

By the late 1950s the whole area around the Creek had become an evil-smelling slum and had to be demolished. Much of it was swept into parts of the Creek itself, infilling it, and, on the site, an industrial estate with access roads was built. Very little is now left of this once lively area; only tantalising glimpses remain if you know what to look for and where it was. It still remains, however, a fascinating link between the two towns of Sittingbourne and Milton Regis.

By the 1990s the Creek was slowly starting to become clean once again and oysters have been found there. On several occasions seals have also been seen in the water, a sign that fish must be returning.

Crown Quay in its heyday with the Rochester-based barge *Lawson* lying alongside.

The last remaining barge warehouse at Crown Quay, 1999. It stands in the grounds of a builder's yard and could be demolished at any time.

An old barge, left forlornly on the banks of the Creek, 1999. What tales it could tell.

Other barges were maintained in a usable condition, like the *Oak*, which called in to the Dolphin Barge Museum Yard for repairs and maintenance in 1983.

The *Celtic*, on the other hand, is in a far worse state of repair, but efforts are being made to bring her back to her former glory. She is shown moored at the Dolphin Barge Museum, 1995.

The former Smeed Dean barge *Persevere* is now moored in Conyer Creek and used as a housebarge. From her lines, her neighbour appears to be a former MGB or MTB, the *Grayling*.

Conyer Creek from the Swale, 1999.

The disused oyster pond at Murston, 1999. Once oyster fishing was a major industry for Miltonians. Their oysters were said to be amongst the finest in the country, even surpassing those world-famous Whitstable oysters. Now the oysters have all but gone, the pond is a haven for wildlife.

Looking across the oyster pond towards Kemsley paper mill, 1999.

Milton Road, known by locals as Cheapside, shortly before its demolition, 1972. This was the road that linked Milton to Sittingbourne.

Looking back down Milton Road to the Wyf of Bath pub, where there is now a roundabout, 1972.

A greatly altered Milton Road, 1999.

Eastbourne Street, off Milton Road, 1972.

New Road as it sweeps round from Milton Road towards Mill Street and Milton Regis, early 1970s. Nearly thirty years on the area remains an undeveloped site.

## *CHAPTER THREE*

# SITTINGBOURNE

Sittingbourne High Street looking eastwards to St Michael's Church, *c.* 1910. From this photograph it can be seen that the better-quality buildings were ranged along the south side. This was because their rears faced on to the more pleasant aspect of fields and open land. Buildings on the north side overlooked the Creek, brickfields and a generally more industrialised landscape.

Sittingbourne is situated on the old Roman road Watling Street and it's this which has made the town what it is today. This was the most important road in Kent until recent times, and it determined Sittingbourne's development right up to the mid-nineteenth century.

Unlike its more wealthy neighbour Milton, Sittingbourne remained a hamlet of little importance until the death of Thomas Becket in 1170. Visits to his tomb became the most popular pilgrimage in Britain as a steady stream of pilgrims made their way along Watling Street. It was not long before the inhabitants of Sittingbourne came to realise a good living was to be made from them. Inns and hostelries sprang up, initially near the church but gradually spreading westwards. By the time Chaucer wrote about one such group of travellers in 1340, the town was well established as a principal place of rest and refreshment along the route, and is one of the few towns actually named in the book.

From such humble beginnings Sittingbourne became an important staging post on the old coaching route, being equidistant between London and Dover – a distance of 71 miles which took the average coach five days to cover. In later years, faster coaches were introduced which could complete the journey in one and a half days with only one overnight stop. That stop was at Sittingbourne. In 1726 George II is reported as having travelled directly from Hythe to Sittingbourne without the customary overnight stop at Canterbury. He was but one of many monarchs who rested in the town; Queen Victoria, then a Princess, was the last when she rested at the Rose Inn on her way back from the continent in the early nineteenth century.

Two streams cross this road on their way to the Creek; of the two, that at the junction of Crown Quay Lane, Bell Road and the High Street seems to be the more important. As at many fords and river crossings, a settlement grew up and it was here the Saxons built their church on a site now occupied by St Michael's Church, which dates back to the eleventh century. On its south-eastern corner is a niche built into a buttress which once held a statue of the Virgin Mary. Here, sheltered by a lean-to structure, the pilgrims would hear mass before continuing their journey.

This statue must have been held in high esteem by locals as there are a couple of instances of them asking to be buried nearby. Robert Wyborn, one of Jack Cade's

St Michael's Church from where the town began, 1908. The shop to the right where the cinema now stands was Boulding's butchers, beside which was Daly's milliners.

rebels, requested in his will of January 1473 'I be buried neare St Marie of the Boterasse'. Similarly, a little earlier in 1466 John Lotter left 6*d* to 'the little chapel of Blessed Mary at Botras'. It's interesting to see how spellings changed in so short a period of time.

The church was almost destroyed by fire in July 1762 when a plumber by the name of Sherwin was repairing the lead roof over the south aisle. He went off for his lunch, leaving a fire burning. Within an hour the whole roof was destroyed and the interior of the church gutted. In the following December an architect reported that the church could be repaired at little cost. After five years' work the building was reopened for worship.

The other ford, at the junction of Ufton Lane, West Street and the main road, had a chapel and hospice in medieval times dedicated to St Thomas. It was built in around 1250 for the use of pilgrims passing through, and was for many years in secular occupation, forming a hamlet called Sittingbourne Parva. It later became known as Schamel and remained a religious site, a convent school, right up to the early 1990s when it was demolished and a housing development built upon the site. It was the nearby paper mills which caused this stream to dry up from the eighteenth century onwards.

The start of St Michael's Road, formerly Cockleshell Walk and before that Water Lane, originally led into a 2 acre plot known as Borden Mead, the site of a house which in the reign of Queen Elizabeth was called Borden House. It was demolished sometime in the fifteenth century. In 1721 Borden Mead belonged to the Earl of Chesterfield, the Lord of Chilton Manor, even though it lies within the Manor of Bayford. To the north of Borden Mead is the paper mill.

Despite its general insignificance, Sittingbourne caught the eye of celebrated horseback traveller Celia Fiennes in 1697 when she wrote of the town: 'this is a very good town for the road and travellers as you shall meete with'. She also noted the great hopfields between Sittingbourne and Faversham which existed until comparatively recent times. When the Kent historian Hasted undertook his survey of Kent in 1778–99 it was not the town as such which caught his eye, but the Rose Inn (now occupied by a Wimpy Bar and Woolworth's) which he described as 'the most superb of any throughout the kingdom'. Of the town he wrote: 'It has a wide, long street, unpaved, the houses of which are mostly modern, being well-built of brick and sashed, the whole having a cheerful aspect. The principal support of it has always been from the inns and houses of reception for travellers of which there are several.'

This was the great age of coach travel, and the town's place in Kent's social and commercial life was at its peak. The town must have been a lively place, with the larger inns keeping sizeable stables for the frequent changes of horses needed for the coaching trade. The George for example, had stabling facilities for forty horses. The innkeepers prospered, and owned land and property in the area.

During this period the novelist Jane Austen frequently passed through on her way from Dartford to Chilham. The town is often mentioned in her letters and it's

Once over Snipeshill, the first major building is the Shire pub, formerly the Shakespeare Hotel. This photograph was taken before Gaze Hill Avenue was built opposite, *c.* 1920s.

interesting to note that on one occasion the journey to Rochester took only an hour and a quarter.

Today most of these old coaching inns and hostelries have long disappeared, the premises being replaced by modern shops. However, if you look carefully you'll see that many such shops have a wide side alley which originally led to the stables at the rear.

Sittingbourne's growth was not without its fair share of problems. Surviving medieval records show that there were several local men involved in Wat Tyler's insurrection against Richard II in the fourteenth century. The revolt followed the introduction of a Poll Tax designed to raise money for a war against the French. Men from all over the south and south-east marched to London in 1381 to demand changes in the agricultural system, which at the time included serfdom, a system under which the peasants were owned by the Lords of the Manor and as such had to spend part of their time working for their Lord for free. Although the rumour is unsubstantiated by genealogical records, I have been told that relatives on my father's side of the family are descended from the notorious Wat Tyler. Perhaps this explains my rebellious nature when dealing with those in authority!

An increasingly unstable royal government in the fifteenth century led to a period of growing anarchy during which the people of Kent suffered enormously from the brutality and oppression of local tyrants like Lord Saye and his son-in-law Sir William Crowmer of Tunstall. In 1450 several Sittingbourne men joined a revolt led by Jack Cade and marched on London, where they beheaded both Saye and Crowmer.

During the Wars of the Roses in 1471 Sittingbourne was caught up in one of its more desperate episodes. Sir Thomas Fauconberg, the illegitimate son of William Nevill, Earl of Kent, marched from Canterbury to London with a mercenary army, intent on freeing Henry VI from the Tower. Fauconberg rested awhile in Sittingbourne from where he sent a letter to the Lord Mayor of London requesting his assistance. It's not known whether any local men joined this mercenary army, but it's a fair assumption that some must have done.

This troubled time and the ensuing Tudor era saw a decrease in the number of pilgrims passing through the town until 1538, when they stopped altogether. The more stable social conditions of the sixteenth century encouraged travel for its own sake.

Sittingbourne being on Kent's principal thoroughfare between Dover and London meant that many English monarchs have rested in the town. Henry V was

As visitors approach the town today, the shops of East Street lie ahead, with the new St Michael's Road taking traffic out of the town centre to their right.

entertained at the Red Lion on his triumphant return from the Battle of Agincourt in 1415. In 1532 Henry VIII brought a retinue of some two thousand to town. It was one of several visits he made, and whilst many of the courtiers stayed in local inns and hostelries, Henry himself would have stayed in one of the local manor houses.

George I and George II often rested here when travelling to and from the continent. They generally stayed at a house now occupied by Blundells furniture shop. In earlier times this imposing three-storey building had been an inn, the George and Dragon. When the Lushington family purchased it in the early eighteenth century they converted it to a town mansion. The remaining George Inn was the original tap house, formerly called the Bell.

By now the townspeople felt Sittingbourne was large enough and important enough to be granted some sort of official status. Their chance to petition Queen Elizabeth came in 1573 when she was staying at Tunstall on her way to Canterbury. She granted the town incorporation, a weekly market and two annual fairs. Incorporation gave a limited degree of self government and the right to raise revenue through a rating system. This was violently quashed by Sir William Crowmer, and the people of Milton protested that the market and fairs would be detrimental to their own ancient privileges. It all came to nothing. In 1579 Crowmer's objection was upheld and a State Decree of Court revoked the granting of the market and fair saying it was prejudicial to that of Milton. However, it was reinstated in the town's second charter of 1599, but only the fairs continued.

The town's history begins to take on a different character from the seventeenth century onwards, when the economic relationship between Sittingbourne and Milton started to change. Milton developed its role as a market town whilst Sittingbourne's was abandoned. The close proximity of the two towns played a leading role in this decision. Being about a mile apart, they are much closer than any other two market centres, the average being nearer to 7 miles. Sittingbourne traders therefore set up stalls in Milton.

Another factor that played an important part in Sittingbourne abandoning its role as a market town was the importance of its inns. They required foodstuffs in bulk for both customers and their horses. Whereas the market stalls could cater for the average household, they would almost certainly not be able to supply goods on a large scale. The inns were, therefore, supplied directly by local farmers who in many cases also owned the inn. Given the special requirements of the inns and the availability of Milton's market for the rest of the population, Sittingbourne seems unique in that it did not need a market as did other towns of a similar size.

The final factor which affected the town's decision not to have a market was that Sittingbourne is a one-street town. The width of the road is fairly uniform throughout its length, which was ideal for the growth of its inns. It allowed for the development of stables and coach houses at the rear with easy access to the High Street. Market stalls in the main road would have restricted the movement of traffic and reduced access to the inns. Clearly this would have been detrimental to the town's main economy.

The English Civil War bypassed Sittingbourne except for one incident. In 1648 a magazine of arms destined for Parliamentary forces was seized in the town. This insurrection, in which Edward Hales of Tunstall played a leading role, culminated in the Battle of Maidstone when the royalists were defeated. In 1688 James II was captured off Faversham whilst fleeing into exile, and was taken to Sittingbourne to await escort to London. According to Daniel Defoe, who wrote about the capture, 'The King was roughly handled by the locals who treated him with the utmost indecency that the King said he was never more apprehensive of his life than at that time.'

The road, which had carved Sittingbourne's place in history, was augmented by the coming of the railway in 1857; it ran initially from Chatham to Faversham. In June the following year a branch line from Sittingbourne to Sheerness was opened. A bridge for both road and rail travellers was constructed at Kings Ferry on the banks of the Swale, linking the island to the mainland for the first time; the railway company charged a toll fee for crossing it. By 1860 the line had been extended from Chatham to Victoria. This increased use of the line led to many improvements at Sittingbourne station, principally a subway beneath the tracks to enable passengers to get from one platform to another in safety. The railway company also applied to take possession of a public road and footpath near the Latimer Chapel in the Butts, so they could extend their site to build a goods yard for livestock and freight.

Looking up the High Street from the Bull Hotel in days gone by.

Since 1800 the town's population has steadily increased from 3,000 to 38,500 in 1991, when the last census was taken. Much of this population explosion can be accounted for by the new paper and brickmaking industries, but when the railway was electrified in 1961 it improved travel to London, and Sittingbourne quickly became a dormitory town for commuters. New estates of houses sprang up all over the town to house these 'incomers' and slowly much of the old agricultural land was lost.

In the early 1970s a major redevelopment plan swung into operation, clearing away many of the derelict slum areas of Sittingbourne and Milton. A new ring road, St Michael's Road, was built, linking the eastern end of the town to the western end, effectively taking through traffic out of the town centre.

How very different it all is now compared with a description written by John Leland in 1546 when he told Henry VIII that 'Sittingburn, alias Sidingbourne, is a prety thorowfare of one parish and by the church renneth a little burne or rille, whereof peradventure the towne toke name'.

Visitors to Sittingbourne travelling on the A2 from the east will notice little difference in this view of Canterbury Road taken in 1920. Only the outlook of the houses has changed. In the 1920s they overlooked rolling fields, but a row of houses was built opposite in the 1930s and the rest of the greenfield land was used to build the Canterbury Road Estate in the early 1960s. This estate was much needed for those displaced by the slum clearance programme taking place in Milton.

East Street, dominated by the white marble frontage of the Co-op departmental store and the Gothic Methodist church, 1971.

The Co-op was demolished in 1994, and with it the highly popular Regis Suite function rooms. It was replaced by a red-brick supermarket, Aldi's, whose entrance is in St Michael's Road, not East Street, demonstrating the preferential treatment of cars over pedestrians. The Methodist church has also been sold and is now a whitewashed sports centre specialising in martial arts.

Visitors approaching from the western end of town will notice even more startling changes. This is Key Street, the crossroads of the A2 and the A249 Sheerness to Maidstone road, in 1981. Key Street was a self-contained community of a pub, shops, a chapel and a couple of garages.

By the early 1990s all had been swept away, as an enormous roundabout and underpass were constructed to replace the old crossroads, and the later small roundabout to ease the traffic flow.

One of the garages managed to survive; this photograph looks towards Sittingbourne, 1999.

The Key Inn sign was saved when the pub at Key Street (opposite, above) was demolished, and is now incorporated into the gate of a nearby cottage.

The shops and pub at Key Street, looking towards Keycol Hill, 1981.

The same view, 1999.

Beyond Key Street, the road to Maidstone has been greatly improved by a dual carriageway leading to the M2 and M20 motorways. The original road lies to the left of the picture.

At the top of Keycol Hill is Keycol Hospital, built in 1880 as an isolation hospital. A sanatorium was later added. In the 1980s it was used as a sports injuries clinic. The mystery is, who is the sentry armed with a walking stick and cap, at a jaunty angle, who the photographer saw fit to place on guard?

One of the major casualties in the building of St Michael's Road was the loss of Sittingbourne Butts. Arthur Tyler, a local chimney sweep who lived in Grafton Road, is pictured here with his grandsons Charlie (sitting on the cart) and Tim (holding the reins). St Michael's vicarage, which was demolished in 1959, can be seen over the wall behind.

As St Michael's Road now sweeps through the Butts, this is where the previous photograph was taken. The building with the Bobcat in front, to the right, can be seen on both pictures.

Between the north side of the Butts and the railway lay the Swimming Baths and the Working Men's Club, formerly the Latimer chapel, seen here in 1910.

Sittingbourne Swimming Baths was built in 1896 at a cost of around £2,000. It was paid for by public subscription, the bulk of the money being met by the family of paper maker Frank Lloyd. It was to be but one of several amenities the Lloyds gave the town. In the winter months the pool was drained, flooring was laid over it, and it was used as a gym as well as for roller skating. In later years it was used for indoor bowling, but the building closed in 1989.

The interior of the Swimming Baths, ready for an important event judging by the way seating is laid out. The date of this sepia-toned print is not known, but it's probably about 1900.

After seventy-odd years the interior has changed little – only the style of the swimming costumes.

Along the western end of the Butts was St Michael's School. Between it and the Baths ran an alley leading to the railway station.

By 1976 motor dealers Swale Motors had taken over the former Working Men's Club. St Michael's Road was in place and the days of the Swimming Baths were numbered.

Today all has gone. The only reminder is that the Swimming Baths once backed on to the railway signal box.

The new leisure centre built to replace the old Swimming Baths is the Swallows in the Avenue of Remembrance. It was officially opened in 1989 by HRH Princess Anne.

An interior view of the Swallows, showing the changes in design that have taken place over a relatively short space of time.

Lloyd's Clubhouse, a sports and social club originally built for those working in the paper mills.

Middle Street, Sittingbourne, overlooking the railway station forecourt. The Fountain Hotel can be seen in the centre. Under the water tank tower was a taxi office, a building used in earlier times as a temporary mortuary for victims of accidents and suicides on the railway.

As St Michael's Road sweeps westward, Middle Street and all the roads and houses between it and the High Street were demolished. The Fountain Hotel can still be seen on the right.

Station Street, connecting the High Street to the railway station, 1974.

Station Street today, with only a few of the original houses and shops remaining on the left-hand side to remind you how it once looked. A new Co-op store and car park occupy all of the right-hand side.

H.J. Sampson's shop, West Street, opposite the junction with Park Road. The premises are now occupied by Telefix Ltd, a TV repair shop; the radio and TV shop next door in the photo is now an Indian restaurant.

Sittingbourne High Street showing the old post office, a site now occupied by Argos. The post office was opened in 1911 and closed in 1961 when new, larger premises were built in Central Avenue. The old post office had formerly been the home of surgeon F. Grayling, and had previously been next to the Bull Hotel for fifteen years, moving in 1892 to larger premises a little further down the High Street to premises near where D&A Toys, formerly Henry S. Tett, now stands. The old post office was considered to be one of the most complete post offices in Kent, with a postbox inside as well as outside the building, a system for handling money orders, and connection to the telegraph system. Behind the main room was a sorting office, employing up to eight staff at the busiest times.

The same scene in 1974 after the post office had been demolished and a parade of shops built on the site. At the time of the photograph, the Co-op on the left was still under construction.

Some time after 1911 the Prudential Assurance Co. purchased a plot of land between the post office and the Baptist church for their new offices. The premises would stand to one side and in front of the three town houses Cedars, Pulveners and The Lawns, which lay behind the trees and which were all demolished in 1988.

The corner of Crescent Street, 1911.

A slightly later view of the corner of Crescent Street, showing the offices of solicitors Winch Greensted & Winch in premises later occupied by Wicks bakers and now Curry's Electrical. David Greig's (now Evans clothes shop) can be seen to the left and down Crescent Street itself is the BRS Haulage Depot, Sittingbourne's original fire station.

The junction of Crescent Street and the High Street is now the entrance to the Forum Shopping Centre. This was how shoppers first saw the Forum in 1974.

The view looking up Crescent Street to the High Street in 1972, shortly before demolition took place in readiness for the new shopping centre. Remember the old school rooms to the right, a civic meeting place before the Town Hall was built?

Inside the newly completed Forum Shopping Centre, 1980. What a contrast to the scene today. Note the claustrophobically low ceiling, concrete benches and generally dismal atmosphere.

Today, with its high, glass roof, the Forum is a much brighter and more pleasant place through which to stroll. Somerfields replaced Key Markets long ago.

In 1983 the shopping centre had no doors, allowing unrestricted access out of hours.

In December 1997 Sittingbourne had a taste of local radio when Bernard Bibby and a team of enthusiasts set up an experimental radio station in an empty shop unit in the Forum. The trial ran for twenty-eight days in accordance with the Radio Authority's licence, and proved to be popular with local residents.

Look at the roofline of the shops between Berry Street and Crescent Street and beyond. It suggests that at one time a far grander building stood here. It is in fact the site of the house and garden of Capt. Vallance, a notable citizen who had several local business interests. Originally the house had been an hotel called the Six Bells, which replaced the even earlier Kings Head of 1630. It stood in half an acre of land. The change in name took place in about 1752. Soon after, it reverted to a private house, and a new house was built in the grounds. The original building was divided between two owners and the old brewhouse became the Poor House, which was later transferred to another former inn, the Gun, which stood opposite the Red Lion.

Sittingbourne Town Hall, 1910. The building was erected in 1859 at a cost of £1,100 and was used as a Corn Exchange until 1879 when it became the Town Hall. The corn market was held each Wednesday, the first being on 12 January 1859. The triple-dialled clock was added to the building in 1860.

The Town Hall was demolished in 1969 and, as it was being torn apart, artist D. Colthup had the presence of mind to capture its image for one last time. Copies of this fine print can be purchased at the Heritage Museum.

The site of the old Town Hall is now occupied by the Nat West bank.

Sittingbourne High Street, 1910. Taylor & Son was a jeweller and silversmith. The shop was later divided between Carlton Café, later Barrows, and Bateman the optician. The pub to the right was the Three Post Boys, later becoming a pet and garden centre. To the left, now the Halifax Building Society, was the London & County Bank which later became the Nat West.

This aerial photograph taken in the 1920s highlights the general layout of the town. St Michael's Church can be seen in the bottom right-hand corner and the railway station in the top right.

The West Street end of town, 1920.

# CHAPTER FOUR
# TRADE & INDUSTRY

Sittingbourne Cattle Market used to be held on alternate Mondays and was said to be one of the best in the county. The site today is a car park beside the DSS offices and in front of the Swallows Leisure Centre.

Until the nineteenth century, Sittingbourne and Milton Regis were in what was predominantly an agricultural area; they were both market towns serving the whole of the Hundred of Milton. Two-thirds of the population were employed in some form of agriculture. Of the two towns, Milton was the centre for fishing, and in the sixteenth century 10 per cent of its population owned a vessel of some description. This was a time when wool was essential to the economy and the Hundred was an area where sheep thrived. There are references to weaving taking place in the two towns, and in Milton there was a saffron garden, which was probably used to dye the wool as well as for culinary use.

In 1952 livestock was still being driven along local lanes and byways on foot, as can be seen in this picture of sheep being driven along The Street in Borden.

As well as fresh agricultural produce, there was also an abundance of fresh meat. Allied to the meat trade was that of tanning, to produce leather after the meat had been stripped from the carcass. There were two tanneries in Milton, both in Chalkwell Road. An important ingredient for tanning is tannic acid which comes from the bark of oak trees, of which there were many throughout the area. It took approximately 300 lbs of oak bark to tan 100 lbs of hide in order to get 150 lbs of leather. As leather was so plentiful, there were ten businesses making boots and shoes in Milton alone in 1862. There were many others making saddles, harness, gun cases, pouches, belts, portmanteaux, leggings, satchels, and many other items.

Another by-product of the meat trade was tallow, which was produced from melted-down animal fats. Candles formed the bulk of artificial light in those days. They were also used by auctioneers as primitive timepieces. Bidders were allotted the space of time it took for a candle to burn down by 1 inch.

Travel to and from Sittingbourne in the nineteenth century was supplemented by Milton Creek, which became a major highway for transporting bricks and cement to London as the capital grew in the wake of the repeal of the Brick Tax in 1850. Buildings of a greater height than ever before were being constructed, and for this stronger bricks were needed. The locally made Kentish stock brick was ideal. At the time it was said to be the most durable brick in the world, and with it were built such notable London buidings as Tower Bridge, Buckingham Palace, the Law Courts, Kings Cross station and Westminster Cathedral, to name but a few. Take a brick from any of these buildings today and you're sure to find it stamped 'SD', standing for Smeed Dean, although some will tell you it stands for Strength and Durability.

The secret of the Kentish stock brick's durability was the way in which it was made. The brick earth was mixed with ash and clinker, mostly from London's rubbish heaps, which were brought back to Sittingbourne by returning barges. When the bricks were fired, the ash and clinker ignited, producing a brick of high tensile strength. How ironic to think that many of London's finest public buildings are made of its own rubbish.

The railway also brought a need for a seemingly inexhaustible supply of bricks as it drew together many of London's suburbs, greatly increasing the size of the capital. Thousands of bricks were needed for the many stations, bridges, tunnels and arches along the new rail routes. At its peak of production over 6,000 people were employed in the local brickworks, making the brickfields and cement works

Sittingbourne railway station, 1909, when the station had a single-span roof and no footbridge for passengers to cross the lines.

one of the largest industrial complexes in southern England. Sittingbourne was ideally situated as a belt of clay runs east to west through the area, from the marshes in the north to just south of the A2 road. Beyond that, the soil becomes chalky as it rises towards the South Downs. And chalk is the main ingredient for cement.

It was during the brickmaking boom that Murston emerged as a separate part of Sittingbourne. It was the centre of operations for George Smeed who employed a large labour force, building over 200 cottages for some of his workers in Murston Road.

Smeed was a shrewd man; his empire was phenomenal. He owned a considerable number of parcels of land around the south and east of the town amounting to 2½ square miles. Here he dug for clay, chalk and flints, as well as building a cement works, a gas works and two barge yards. They were served by over a mile of wharfage. His landholdings were managed by George Dean, a young farmer who later married Smeed's eldest daughter, Mary Ann. In 1875 the two men consolidated their interests to become a private limited company, Smeed Dean & Co. Ltd. This partnership worked well, and when all the brick earth had been extracted from the land, the fields were returned to agricultural use to continue making a profit. Unlike many other industries which extract raw materials from the ground, brick earth extraction did not affect the landscape and its original use could be restored within a few years. The only clue left to remind you of the field's former industrial use was that it was some 6 to 8 ft lower than the road.

The building boom declined after the First World War, and with it the brick-making industry. The once vast brickfields have now all been developed into modern industrial trading estates, leaving few clues of their former use.

With economical and speedy travel links by road, rail and barge in place, papermaker Edward Lloyd looked to the town in 1863 as an ideal place to which to move his rapidly expanding papermaking business from Boxbridge on the outskirts of London. Edward Lloyd supplied the paper for his *Lloyd's Weekly London Newspaper*. This was not the first paper mill to be situated in the town, however. Local parish registers of 1737 show that at this time there was a paper mill in Sittingbourne run by the Archer family. Whereas Edward Lloyd's process involved the use of straw and esparto grass, Robert Archer's used rags. By 1752 the mill was owned by William Stevens, and by the beginning of the 1800s by Edward Smith. It was he who let the mill fall into disuse by 1850. It has been suggested that this was because Edward Smith tried to progress from handmade paper to machine-made, but the machines were difficult to operate without highly skilled labour. Another theory is that the new railway line was scheduled to run alongside the mill. Edward Smith objected on the grounds that this would make the mill useless for papermaking: the smoke and dust from the railway would have ruined the paper which needs a clean atmosphere. His objection was over-ruled and the mill closed down. Edward Lloyd eagerly snapped up the site.

Initially the Sittingbourne mill supplemented Edward Lloyd's Boxbridge plant, but in 1863, soon after being purchased, the old Sittingbourne mill was destroyed by

Two views from Murston Quay looking north and south, 1999: a mere shell of its former busy self.

fire. In 1866 work began on a new, much larger mill near the old site, but closer to the railway. It produced 50 tons of paper a week, compared to the 36 tons produced at Boxbridge. The census of 1871 shows it employed six paper makers, one printer and five labourers as well as Edward Lloyd's son Frank, who was the paper mill overlooker.

Edward Lloyd purchased the *Daily Chronicle* newspaper in 1876, and began slowly to increase the size of operations at Sittingbourne. By 1882 management of the mill had been taken on by Edward's younger son Frederick Lloyd and the full papermaking process was transferred from the London plant. Unlike the brick and cement industries which had faced problems in the early part of the twentieth century, the papermaking industry enjoyed a period of growth development. This was because of the efforts of Edward Lloyd and his eldest son Frank who were at the forefront of new developments. One such move was to use imported wood pulp rather than straw.

By the time of the First World War Edward Lloyd's operation had expanded to include a dock for ocean-going vessels at Ridham, on the Swale near Kings Ferry Bridge. It was linked to the Sittingbourne mill by a railway. He also purchased a Norwegian wood-pulping plant.

In 1918 Frank Lloyd, now in charge of the business, sold off the newspapers his family owned to concentrate on general paper making. They were sold to United Newspapers Ltd, and part of the deal was that Lloyds would supply all of their newsprint for the next thirty years.

In the 1920s there was a shortage of wood pulp and an increased demand for paper. The cost of paper rose rapidly. As the demand for paper exceeded the capacity of the Sittingbourne mill, despite its workers working twenty-four hours a day in three shifts, it was decided to build a second mill. With no room on the existing site, land was purchased at Kemsley, to the north of Milton. Work began in 1923, and by the following year the new mill was fully functional.

No doubt influenced by new garden towns which were springing up all over the country, Frank Lloyd built a village for his workers, Kemsley. It was designed to house 3,500 and by the summer of 1927, 188 of the planned 750 houses had been built. Kemsley is no longer reserved for paper mill workers. The area has been expanded by modern development, and even the playing fields have been built upon.

Between them, the two mills employed over 2,000 people and the company was the largest employer in the area. Following the death of Frank Lloyd in 1927, the business was sold to Berry's who owned Allied Newspapers – to whom Frank Lloyd had sold his newspapers in 1918. Sir William Berry told his shareholders that the Sittingbourne and Kemsley plants between them were the largest in the country and larger than any in the USA or Canada. The annual output was 200,000 tons of newsprint.

Despite being the major employer in the town and bringing wealth and prosperity to the area, the paper mill was not without its fair share of critics. Just

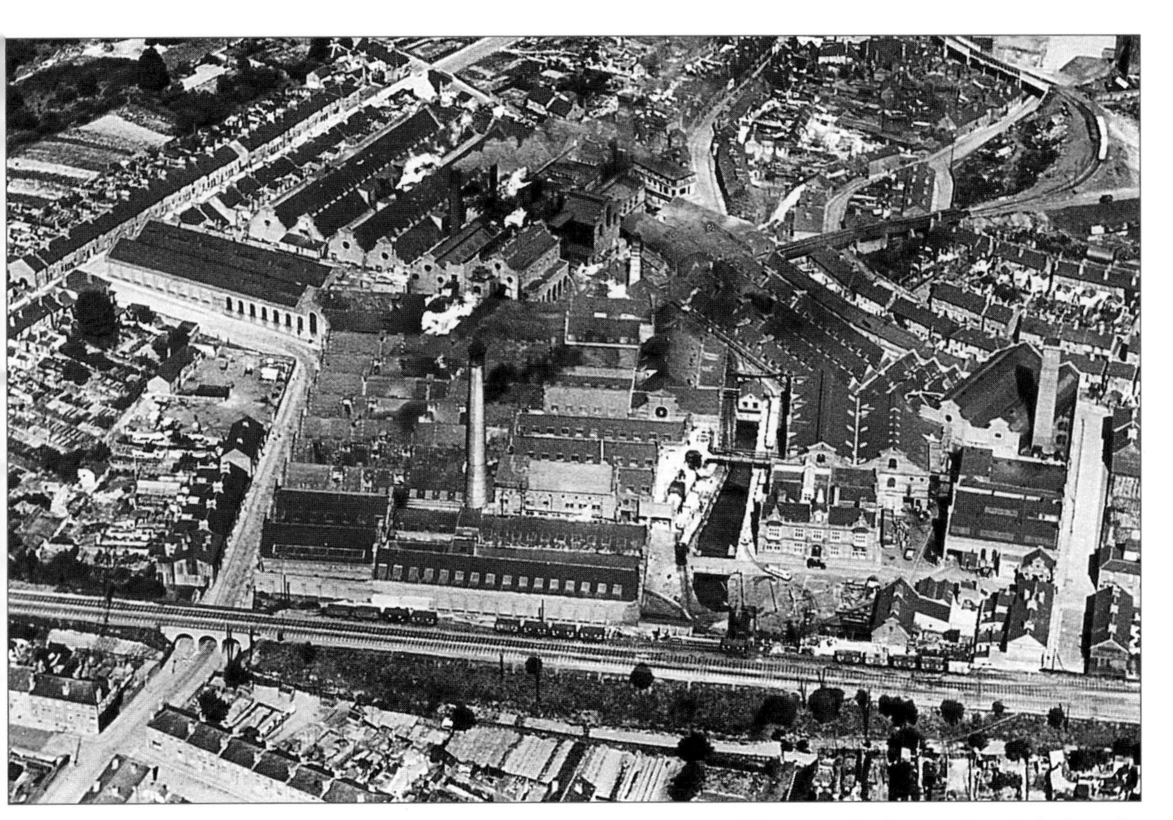

An aerial view of Lloyd's paper mill, 1920s. Many of the old streets and houses which were demolished in the slum clearance programme programme of the mid-1970s can clearly be seen.

as the importance of the position of Sittingbourne on Watling Street and its location in relation to London had affected the town's development, so too had the position of Milton on Milton Creek affected its economic growth as a fishing port. The Creek began its decline when Edward Lloyd's paper mill began operating.

Papermaking requires vast amounts of water and the natural flow from the Periwinkle stream soon became inadequate. Wells were sunk to extract supplies from lower down in the sub-strata. Milton Creek was slowly robbed of its natural flow of pure water essential to the survival of shellfish, and gradually became the polluted, silted-up waterway we have today.

As early as the nineteenth century, complaints were being lodged about the pollution from the mill chimneys. Milton residents petitioned the mill owners about the smoke, fine ashes and sulphuric fumes which were being showered all over the town. The mill blamed the inferior quality of the coal it had had to purchase during a coal crisis up north. In 1895 the townspeople again complained, this time about the foul smell from the Creek during hot weather. Despite the Milton Creek Conservancy Board being set up to control the Creek, little was done and as recently as 1952 complaints about the 'bad egg-like smell' were still being made. In

The Bargeman statue erected in the High Street to commemorate Sittingbourne's links with the barge industry.

1974 a survey of the pollution was a winner in a National Environment Competition: the survey found Milton Creek to be the worst polluted area in the south of England.

Perhaps it's unfair to lay all the blame of Milton Creek's decline on the paper mill, even if it was a major contributor. The decline in maritime traffic after the demise of the barge trade is another significant factor. With less use and no fast-flowing stream, the Creek could do little else but to slowly silt up.

Milton Creek and its assorted trades were not the only casualties of the new paper mill. The town's watermills also suffered from the acute shortage of water. The Domesday Book recorded that there were six such mills in Milton in 1086. Writing at the end of the eighteenth century, Hasted noted Sittingbourne had four corn mills and Periwinkle mill, which was used to produce pearl barley. This latter mill continued working up to the nineteenth century, when all the others had long ceased.

Periwinkle Mill was the middle one of three mills which stood on the mile-long Periwinkle stream. This surfaced in Cockleshell Walk, ran through the paper mill and ran into the Creek at Flushing Street. The mill stood in Church Street for over

One of the deserted and derelict paper storage sheds near the terminus of the Sittingbourne & Kemsley Light Railway, 1999.

400 years. When the mill stopped working it was purchased by the Hales family who had a butcher's shop there until the 1960s. The mill house was totally derelict, and by 1968 was in such a dangerous condition that it had to be demolished. Much of the mill machinery remained, and with the owner's consent, the Sittingbourne Society sought ways in which it could be restored to form a centrepiece of a museum. After a feasibility study, the project got under way in 1985, when it was Commended in the Civic Trust's prestigious 'Pride of Place' competition. In 1990, after much voluntary and professional help from many individuals and local firms, the Royal Engineers installed the waterwheel, hurst frame (which supports the millstones) and major machinery. When the new wheel was turned for the first time, the gears meshed perfectly. Phase One of the project was completed. Phase Two consists of the construction of the main museum building, which requires a lot of money.

Bell Road looking towards the High Street, 1975, showing Packers basket shop and Featherstone's, beyond which is the rear of the Three Kings pub on the corner with East Street.

Featherstone's departmental store, 1937.

The Rose & Crown, which stood almost opposite Featherstone's, is now an Indian restaurant. Could this have been the darts team off to another match?

Bell Road, 1999. Both shops have been demolished and replaced by a car park.

West Street, *c.* 1900.

West Street, 1970s.

The Volunteer pub in West Street, just before it closed in 1972. In earlier times the pub had been named the Seven Stars, the Cherry Tree and the Union Flag. When it was known as the Cherry Tree, the road outside was called Cherry Tree Hill.

After many years the Convent School on the corner of Ufton Lane and West Street was demolished and a block of flats built on the site. Houses were built on the old playing field at the rear.

Those early postcard photographers must have had a keen sense of humour. This postcard is entitled 'Lloyd's Paper Mill by moonlight' but a paper mill does not readily spring to mind when you think of subjects to photograph by moonlight.

The entrance to UK Paper today.

Murston's original thirteenth-century church. Murston Old Church is dedicated to All Saints. This building is typically early English in design, having been built in the late twelfth/early thirteenth centuries. It originally had three chancels, a nave with a transept on each side, and a square tower with a wooden turret containing three bells. As the village of Murston grew in size with all the industrial activity of brick making, cement production, the gas works and the numerous wharves and quays, the original building became inadequate to hold all the congregation. In 1873/4 the Rector of Murston, Revd Hoare, had the church pulled down except for the centre chancel, and erected a new larger church on the site. The last service to be held in the old church was in July 1874. What we have left today is the original centre chancel, and few traces of the old church remain.

The former Brickmaker's Arms pub just off the former Murston Quay. This quay served those working in the nearby gas works, cement works and brickfields, so together with the barge crews, what a centre this must have been for so many diverse trades.

A Sittingbourne & Kemsley Light Railway steam train taking visitors on a nostalgic trip across Milton marshes to Kemsley Down. This was the railway line originally set up to transport men and materials between Sittingbourne and Kemsley paper mills and Ridham Dock. In October 1969, as road transport had taken over much of the railway's workload, the line became surplus to requirements and was offered to the Light Railway Club of Great Britain for a peppercorn rent.

A nostalgic shot of an old steamer pulling out of Sittingbourne station, 1950s.

## *CHAPTER FIVE*

# PLACES LONG GONE

The Ferry Inn at Elmley, a hamlet on the banks of the Swale which is now long gone.

There are several areas around Sittingbourne and Milton Regis which have disappeared altogether with the passing of time. The Creek itself has changed enormously but is basically still there to be seen. Other areas are long gone and remain but a memory in the minds of older residents.

Typical of this is Elmley Ferry to the north of Murston. Originally this small hamlet was the main crossing point from the mainland to the Isle of Sheppey, and at low tide you can still see traces of the old causeway. At high tide the Swale was almost a mile wide, but only 20 ft at low tide. I can remember the derelict Ferry Inn from where the ferrymen once operated three boats. In its heyday there were a set of barge blocks, a boatbuilding shed, a duckpond and two cottages. Today there is nothing left apart from the causeway, and if you want to cross to the island you have to drive to Kings Ferry Bridge further along the Swale.

The site of Elmley's Ferry Inn, 1999. Only the track remains to serve as a reference point.

At the turn of the century the Sheppey hamlet of Elmley on the opposite bank was quite large, consisting of a pub, a church, a school and several cottages. It also had a cement works which closed in 1904, sounding the death knell for the village. Many of the villagers moved to Murston, finding work in the new Smeed Dean brickfields and cement works.

Despite Elmley having a coastguard cutter, smuggling was rife in this bleak, somewhat desolate area. Many of the old footpaths leading back to Bapchild on the A2 road are former smugglers' paths.

The ferry service was in use until shortly after the Second World War when one of the last ferrymen, Jack Carrier, died. The powers that be decided the ferry did not warrant keeping and the boats were taken away. The other ferryman, Jack Wade, lived in his cottage until flooded out in 1953, when an exceptionally high spring tide swept along the whole of the east coast of Britain. He moved to Murston, and Elmley Ferry, like its neighbour Elmley, became derelict. Later that same year a scrap metal dealer moved on to the site, bringing with him two old minesweepers whose wrecks can still be seen there today. The old Ferry Inn was finally demolished in the early 1960s. The area is now part of a nature reserve which is popular with bird watchers.

Other long-gone areas of the towns include the brickworks, cement works, barge yards, and country houses belonging to the industrialists who grew rich on these new industries. Typical of the latter is Gore Court, once the home of George Smeed. It was an attractive mansion with elegant pillars supporting the roof of the front veranda, which was originally owned and rebuilt in 1791 by Mr Gabriel Harper. After Smeed's death in 1881 the building had a variety of uses, including being a school and military hospital. It was demolished in 1926, and in 1937 the parkland in which it stood opened to the public as King George's Playing Field. All that now remains of this once elegant house are the bases of the pillars and the present pavilion, which was originally the stable block. One way to approach King George's today is by Park Avenue, earlier known as Tunstall Avenue, which was the original driveway to the house.

Another long-gone country mansion is Woodstock Park, a manor which at one time was owned by the Benedictine monastery of Minster, Sheppey. The house was built by Sir Abraham Chambers in 1780. In 1945 Woodstock Farm and 250 acres of land were sold at auction to Shell Research. The house lay empty and derelict for many years, being used by the local Civil Defence for training purposes. It was finally demolished in the 1960s. Shell Research vacated the site in the late 1980s.

One of our finest cricket pitches is at The Grove near Key Street, but how many know that at one time this was the site of the front of another great mansion, which stood back amongst the trees behind the present pavilion? We have Mr George Andrews, another local industrialist, to thank for this.

Another of Sittingbourne's great houses once stood near the bottom of Bell Road. It was Trotts Hall, a name later given to an estate of houses built on the corner of Bell Road and the Avenue of Remembrance. It was home to Mr Rex Boucher who, in 1976, seeing modern developments encroaching on him, moved the building brick by brick to

Woodstock Farm and 250 acres of land were sold at auction for £24,000 in 1945 to Shell Research, who slowly developed the site into a large complex of offices, laboratories and social amenities for their staff. They moved out in the late 1980s and the complex was purchased by another firm.

One of Sittingbourne's finest cricket grounds is The Grove near Key Street. It was once the front of a large house, which stood back in the trees. The Grove was given to the people of Sittingbourne by local industrialist George Andrews. (Picture courtesy of H. Wyld)

the more idyllic setting of Milsted Manor. The delicate operation was undertaken by local builders H. Butcher. Mr Boucher originally came from a farming family but it was his business acumen which outshone all else. In the late 1920s he purchased Hulburd's grocery and drapery shop which he developed into a highly successful departmental store. Fifty years later he leased land at the rear of the shop to supermarket supremo J. Sainsbury, and was instrumental in developing the Bell Centre.

At one time Sittingbourne had three cinemas. At first films were shown in all manner of public halls and rooms, but in 1910 the old Wesleyan School building in East Street was converted to become a proper cinema. It was known as the Empire Picture Hall. Two years later, in 1912, the former Vallance & Payne brewery in the High Street was similary converted and called the Queen's Picture Hall. By 1934 the Empire had changed names to the Plaza. The Odeon was built in 1937 on the corner of Crown Quay Lane and the High Street, not the best of places as it was on the old watercourse of the Bourne Stream. During torrential downpours of rain the front stalls of the cinema were often flooded.

Two factors greatly affected cinema audiences in the 1960s – television and bingo. The Plaza had closed down sometime in the late 1950s/early 1960s and the site was sold to the Council. The building was ultimately demolished and houses built on the site. There were plans afoot in 1966 for the Odeon to change to a full-time bingo hall. The Council opposed this and later that year the cinema was sold to Classic Cinemas. There was talk of it becoming a gambling casino, but following

The Plaza cinema shortly before its demolition in 1975 to make way for a block of houses to be called Plaza Court.

Hot on the heels of the Empire cinema came the Queens in 1912, built in the former Vallance & Payne brewery off the High Street, up the alley beside Blundell's toy shop. Both cinemas were showing silent films until 'talkies' came along in 1930, when the Queens showed Sittingbourne's first, *Broadway Melody*. With the advent of TV and bingo in the 1960s interest in the cinema greatly dwindled. The Queens closed as a cinema in the early 1970s after over half a century of showing films. By the late 1980s the fire-ravaged building was demolished. Today the site is part of the car park which lies behind the shops.

modernisation and refurbishment it became the Vogue Bingo Hall. Three years later a new cinema opened upstairs. In 1972 actor Richard Hearne, aka Mr Pastry, came to town to open a second cinema in the same building.

After being a cinema for over half a century, the Queens took on a variety of different roles after it stopped showing films in the early 1970s. In 1975 it became a variety theatre, but in the face of spiralling debts closed down after less than a year. After a £40,000 programme of rebuilding in 1980, it re-opened as a cabaret and dining nightclub called Club Cleo. Within three months that too was doomed to failure and the building again closed its doors. It was sold and the next venture – an American-styled discotheque called 'Marteens' – fared little better, lasting six months. Shortly afterwards the building was gutted by fire and plans were announced that it would be turned into an up-market entertainment centre. This venture ran for a couple of years, but in 1984 the building was once again ravaged by fire. It was subsequently sold, but the new owner's plans came to nothing and the building was eventually demolished in the late 1980s. The Queens stood at the end of an alley which is opposite Iceland's freezer supermarket. How many remember the Queens Laundry which stood to the left of that alley?

Finally, we must not forget a great building which was at one time the centrepiece of Sittingbourne High Street, the Town Hall. It was originally erected as the Corn Exchange in 1859. Twenty years later it became the Town Hall and was demolished in 1961 to make way for Central Avenue. The clock which for many years stood in the clock tower above the Town Hall was later mounted in a brick tower outside the new Civic Centre in Central Avenue.

The clock from the old Town Hall, which for so long had informed shoppers of the time, outside the new Civic Centre.

Rodmersham Green, 1909, looking very much as it has done for many centuries. It is typical of the many villages surrounding Sittingbourne.

In the early 1960s Rodmersham's windmill was demolished after much protest and violent demonstrations, with locals chaining themselves to the old building to prevent the demolition squad moving in. A house was later built on the site. The mill had been operating up until the 1920s when the sails were removed. It was hoped the mill would again be used in later years, but it never was. It stood derelict for many years and during the Second World War was used as a look-out post by the Royal Observer Corps. With the exception of the windmill, the skyline looks exactly the same now as it did in 1909. Many ask what became of the donkeys which used to graze on the Green.

Milsted, 1936, is another village little affected by the passing of time.

Woodstock Park, built in 1780, was the home of the Twopenny family. The house became derelict in the 1950s and was used for training purposes by the Civil Defence Corps. It was demolished in the late 1960s.

Today nothing remains of this once fine Georgian mansion. The site has been ploughed over but this is where I think it once stood.

Trotts Hall House, an eighteenth-century mansion which stood at the bottom of Bell Road, Sittingbourne, for many years. It was the home of Mr Rex Boucher, a local farmer who, in the late 1920s, moved into commercial business by purchasing Hulburd's grocery and drapery shop in the High Street. At first he and his wife lived over the shop, turning it into a highly successful departmental store. In the 1970s he leased land at the back of his shop to J. Sainsbury and was instrumental in the development of the Bell Shopping Centre. With so much development taking place and encroaching upon the land around Trotts Hall House, he had the old house dismantled brick by brick and rebuilt at Milsted Manor Farm some miles away. The work was carried out by local builder H. Butcher. (Picture courtesy of the *East Kent Gazette*)

The site of Trotts Hall House today, replaced by an unimpressive office block. The nearby estate of houses is named Trotts Hall Gardens.

Sittingbourne Football Ground, the home of the 'Brickies', has been in use since 1890. This view of the ground was taken from the top of Thames House in Roman Square. In 1985, facing a £20,000 quote to improve safety at their ground as new regulations were introduced for all football clubs, Sittingbourne FC announced plans to sell the Bull ground and move to a new purpose-built stadium at Murston. The club moved to Central Park in 1991.

An eager buyer for the abandoned football ground was J. Sainsbury, keen to move their supermarket from the Bell Centre to larger premises. This is how the old football ground looks today.

The car park of Sittingbourne FC was, for many years, home to Sittingbourne market. We might not have got one when we petitioned Queen Elizabeth I in 1579, but we definitely have now! The market is currently held in the Forum car park.

The old market is now the car park for the supermarket.

## *CHAPTER SIX*

# OF THIS & THAT

A class photograph of the Wesleyan school in East Street, Sittingbourne, pre-1910. In 1909, when the Sittingbourne Council school opened, forcing the closure of many of the town's smaller schools, the Wesleyan was converted to become Sittingbourne's first cinema, the Empire, which changed its name to the Plaza in 1937.

This final chapter consists of photographs which do not readily fit into previous chapters, but will, I hope, bring back memories to readers. It's very much a miscellany and hotchpotch of photographs covering all manner of topics.

I hope you've enjoyed wandering down Memory Lane with me and that this book has evoked some fond memories of yesteryear. With the aid of photographs old and new, I have tried to highlight some of the many changes, both subtle and major, which have taken place in both Sittingbourne and Milton Regis over the years. Many changes have taken place in the past thirty years and even more are in the pipeline. I hope they will be the basis of my next book highlighting the development of Sittingbourne and Milton Regis.

Borden Grammar School was founded as a boys' grammar school for both boarders and day pupils by the Barrow Trustees in 1873. Under the provisions of the will of a local farmer, William Barrow, money was left for the well-being of local people. The building cost around £11,000 and stood in a 7-acre greenfield site, now on the corner of College Road and Riddles Road. After a new, larger building was opened nearer to the centre of Sittingbourne, the old building became the Kent Farm Institute and later the Adult Education Centre.

The new Borden Grammar School in the Avenue of Remembrance, which was officially opened by Lord Harris of Belmont on 4 October 1929.

A group of Borden Grammar School pupils relaxing on the playing field, 1958. Left to right: Bill Burnett, Malcolm Allen, Mick Wheeler, John Golding and John Clancy. Albany Road is in the background and the headmaster's house lies to the left.

The Girls Grammar School was initially at Brenchley House in Sittingbourne High Street and was set up under the terms of the Education Act of 1902. Originally called the County School, it opened in October 1904 and in 1906 amalgamated with the Sittingbourne High School for Girls, which had been next door at no. 77 since the 1890s.

A little-seen view of the rear of Brenchley House. Originally it opened on to the playing fields, but now it overlooks the Swallows Leisure Centre car park.

The Girls Grammar School today in Highsted Road, next door to the Memorial Hospital, which opened in 1958.

Because of climatic changes and the so-called 'greenhouse effect', winters never seem to be as harsh now as many remember they used to be. The last severe winter in Sittingbourne was in 1988 when a considerable amount of snow fell.

Carnival time in Sittingbourne has long been a popular event. The first carnival procession is reported as having taken place in 1893. This is a float entered by the Billet pub in the 1970s.

St Giles' Church, Tonge, is an early Norman building of the thirteenth century, and lies beyond Murston to the east of the town.

Tonge Mill used to be a bakery run by the Wicks family, who had a shop on the corner of Crescent Street and the High Street, Sittingbourne for many years. The mill has two dates on it, 1837 and 1866, so perhaps the original building was later extended. In the 1950s the pond was used as a boating lake, but during the exceptionally hot summers of the 1970s it was feared the pond would be lost as it dried up and the clay lining cracked. Fortunately it was saved before it was too late.

Cheke Court, Tonge, 1999.

Murston Quay approach road with Milton church just visible in the background. As the Eurolink Industrial Estate stretches along the banks of the Creek, many of the old quays are now unapproachable. Murston Gasworks once stood to the right of this picture.

Looking across the Stockbury Valley to the village of Stockbury, 1995. Stockbury Church can just be seen on the brow of the hill.

Heart's Delight, Borden, 1995.

An atmospheric view of Sittingbourne High Street.

# ACKNOWLEDGEMENTS

I would like to thank the following people for lending me their treasured photographs and postcards, and in some cases for giving me free access to their family albums. Without their co-operation this book would not have been possible.

Special thanks are extended to Fred Atkins who lent me his entire collection of photographs of Sittingbourne and Milton Regis for a period of many months, giving me *carte blanche* to use them as I wished. Another key player in the production of this book is Barry Kinnersley, who helped me locate many of the long-gone sites and photographed them before all traces were irrevocably erased.

To everyone who helped, no matter whether in a major or minor way, I would like to record my sincerest thanks:

Mrs K. Mortiboys, Mrs M. McCallum, Mr J. Moys, Mrs Earnshaw, *East Kent Gazette*, Mr and Mrs R. Buck, Mrs R. Ash, Mr T. Fallon, Mr F. Littlewood, Mr K. Washford, Swale Borough Council, Mr H. Wyld, Mr D. Belsom, Mr C. Deamer, Mr and Mrs M. Clancy, Mrs M. Mullins, Mrs M. Fosbray, Mr C. Sampson, Mr P. Ransome-Wallis, Mr D. Colthup.